crafty
girl

fun & games

# crafty girl

# fun & games

## things to make and do

*by Jennifer Traig*

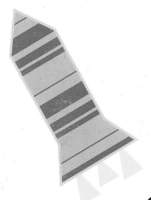

**CHRONICLE BOOKS**

SAN FRANCISCO

Library of Congress Cataloging-in-Publication Data available.
ISBN 0-8118-3125-6

Printed in Singapore

Line drawings by Stephanie Sadler
Designed and illustrated by Gayle Steinbeigle

Distributed in Canada by Raincoast Books
9050 Shaughnessy Street
Vancouver, British Columbia V6P 6E5

10  9  8  7  6  5  4  3  2  1

Chronicle Books LLC
85 Second Street
San Francisco, California 94105

www.chroniclebooks.com

**Notice: This book is intended as an educational and informational guide. With any craft project, check product labels to make sure that the materials you use are safe and nontoxic. "Nontoxic" is a description given to any substance that does not give off dangerous fumes or contain harmful ingredients (such as chemicals or poisons) in amounts that could endanger a person's health.**

# acknowledgments

Thanks to my parents for encouraging crafty fun in the first place, and to my sister Victoria for playing along; to the staff and students at Woodland Montessori Children's House for their generosity with ideas and input; to Mikyla Bruder for being a superlative editor and friend; to Jodi Davis for keeping everything on track; and to Stephanie Sadler, Gayle Steinbeigle, and the rest of the Chronicle crew.

# table of contents

*Y*ou're a Crafty Girl. "Fun" is your middle name and "Games" is your second middle name. You don't even know the meaning of the word "bored." You never run out of ideas, and you never stop looking for new ones. That's where *Crafty Girl: Fun & Games* comes in, with loads of ideas for crafty good times.

You already know that fun is more fun when you make it yourself. Sure, board games are okay, but an Autobiographical Board Game (page 52), a game you've made to reflect *your* world, is a riot. Twister is fun, but do-it-yourself Twist and Shout (page 50) is extremely fun. On family road trips, car bingo is mildly entertaining, but Custom Car-Bingo (page 56) really makes the miles fly by. A game is not really fun for you unless you've colored, cut, and pasted it yourself.

This is not to say you're spending all day hunched over cardboard and crayons. You have as much fun outdoors as you do indoors. The recipes in "Part 1: Fresh Air Fun" will help you do just that. You can transform your yard into a Magical Mini-Golf (page 16) course or a launching pad for your Seltzer Sputnik (page 25). You can get the whole neighborhood together for a Crafty Scavenger Hunt (page 31). When you've got a light wind, a paper bag, and a spare half-hour on your hands, you can Go Fly a Kite (page 22).

Even when the skies are stormy, you forecast fun. The projects in "Part 2: Rainy Day Doings" will cure your cabin fever. Transform any corridor into a lane for Soda Bottle Bowling (page 38), a field for Hallway Croquet (page 41), or a course for the Light-as-a-Feather Foam Glider (page 36). Try all these events at once for an afternoon of indoor Olympics.

Maybe your thing is cloak-and-dagger crafts, or maybe most of your crafting is done in the lab. "Part 3: Spy Supplies and Mad Scientist

Materials" will provide the top-secret recipes you need to get the job done. Make secret agent surveillance tools like Cryptology Crafts (page 68) or Counterintelligence Booby Traps (page 72). Synthesize substances previously unknown to humankind, like Sparkle Slime (page 76) and Shape-Shifting Ooey-Goo (page 78). Is the world ready for these crafty chemical creations? You'll have to make them to find out.

An artsy Crafty Girl does a little time in the painting, drawing, and sculpting department, too. You're so crafty, you make your own craft supplies, and the recipes in "Part 4: Color Chemistry" will show you how. Need paint? Whip up a batch of Whirlwind Watercolors (page 84), Fast-Food Finger Paints (page 86), or Puffy Paint (page 94). Need clay? Cook up a pound of Play Clay (page 88) in an instant. Color you crafty.

Here's a universal truth: Fun is more fun when it's frosted. The recipes in "Part 5: Kitchen Chaos" will let you play with your food. Craft yourself a creative snack like Sugar Glass (page

106) or Invent Your Own Ice Cream (page 111). If your tastes run to snips, snails, and puppy dog tails rather than sugar, spice, and everything nice, you'll find plenty to chew on, too. Mix up some Fudge Sludge (page 108), Swamp Cake (page 113), or Banana Slugs (page 115). If your friends think it's gross, all the better—more for you.

*Crafty Girl: Fun & Games* has a heap of ideas for you, no matter what kind of Crafty Girl you are—even if you're a Crafty Boy, a Crafty Woman, or a Crafty Man. Even if you're a Crafty Pet (be warned, however, that most of these projects require opposable thumbs, so if you're a dog, a cat, or a hamster, you're going to have to ask your master for help with the scissors). If you're a Crafty Babysitter, this book should be part of your emergency entertainment kit. The kids will be so busy with Bubble Brew (page 27), you'll have plenty of free time to raid the fridge and run up the phone bill, but you probably won't want to—you'll be more tempted to blow a few bubbles yourself.

So, what are you waiting for? You have most of the necessary supplies in the house right now. What you don't have, you can find in any supermarket or office-supply store. Most projects call for nothing fancier than cardboard, construction paper, and creativity. The only specialty store you may need to visit is a cake decorating-supply store, for food coloring paste, which is much more vibrant than the stuff you get in the supermarket, and comes in a rainbow of shades (if you don't have a cake decorating emporium in your area, you can easily find one online).

You may also need to go to a craft store for a few supplies, like craft foam and acrylic paint. It's a good idea to peruse a craft store even if your craft cupboard is well stocked. Craft stores are treasure troves of inspiration. You'll come home with one small purchase and two thousand ideas, or if you're like us, you'll come home with two thousand purchases and one small twinge of guilt for buying so much. But we're crafty—we're worth it.

Before we begin, a word of caution. It's all fun and games until someone gets hurt. Most of these projects carry no greater risk than a paper cut, but some of them get hot and some of them get pointy. You'll need to use adult supervision, care, and common sense. The cardinal rules: (1) If it's hot or sharp, don't touch it. (2) Keep it out of your eyes and, unless it's food, out of your mouth. (3) Be sure to have an adult present for any project involving a stove, a cutting knife, or chemicals. Nothing ruins the fun faster than an injury, so be careful.

**Let the games begin!**

part 1

fresh air fun

# magical

## mini-golf

Some things are more fun when they're tiny and cute. Golf is one of them. Make a cardboard course, and you can have big-time mini-golf fun in your own backyard. If it's raining, and your parents aren't worried about the antiques, you can play inside, too. Fore!

### You will need:

Masking tape

2 pieces of cardboard, each 1½ by 4 inches

Yardstick

Tempera or acrylic craft paint and paintbrush (optional)

Scissors

Posterboard or craft foam

Found items to use as hazards: stuffed animal, doll, dollhouse, toy-car race-track, LEGO construction, or whatever else you have on hand

Materials to make hazards: cardboard, milk cartons, shoeboxes, construction paper, cardboard tubes from paper towel rolls, paint, paper glue, or whatever you'd like

Golf ball

[1] Make your golf club by taping your two 1½-by-4-inch pieces of cardboard to the end of your yardstick, one on each side. Secure with more tape as necessary. It ain't cute, but it'll work. If you want cute, paint over the cardboard and tape.

[2] Make your nine holes. For each, cut a circle 6 inches in diameter out of posterboard or craft foam. Cut a smaller circle 2 inches in diameter out of the middle of the 6-inch disk. You should end up with something that looks like a big doughnut. Repeat eight more times for a total of nine holes.

continued on next page

[3] Find or make nine hazards, obstacles that you'll place before the holes. Here's where you get wacky. Anything with a passage big enough to golf through will work, and the funkier it is, the better. Golf through the legs of your blowup Gumby doll or your model horse collection. Set up your Mousetrap game and golf through that. Golf down a toy-car racetrack. Golf over a LEGO construction. Make your own hazards from cardboard, construction paper, and craft paint. Some ideas:

- Make a pyramid by taping four cardboard triangles together. First draw bricks and hieroglyphics. Cut a little tunnel through the bottom so you can golf through it.
- Make a slide for your golf ball to roll down by cutting a paper towel tube in half lengthwise.
- Make a "pond" out of blue or green Sparkle Slime (recipe on page 76) on plastic wrap. Decorate with construction-paper lily pads.

- Make a windmill by covering a milk carton with construction paper and gluing a pinwheel to the side. Cut a tunnel through the bottom.
- Make a house out of a shoebox. Cut a tunnel from one side through to another.
- Make an Eiffel Tower out of cardboard. Golf through the legs.
- Make trees from paper towel tubes and construction paper. Set them up in a zigzag and golf through an obstacle forest.
- Make a castle by covering an oatmeal canister in construction paper. Tape construction-paper cones to the top to make turrets. Cut a tunnel through the bottom. Surround tunnel with a "moat" of blue Sparkle Slime on plastic wrap.
- Make a "desert island" sand trap by filling a pie pan with sand and decorating with construction-paper palm trees.

[4] Set up your Magical Mini-Golf course any way you'd like, put on your loudest pants, tee up your golf ball, and swing away. Whoever gets to the ninth hole with the fewest strokes and the tackiest trousers wins.

# footbag fun

Your feet are itching for some footbag fun, but you don't
have a sack to hack. Make your own! You already have
all the supplies, so what are you waiting for? Hop to it!

**You will need:**

3 balloons

Funnel

1/3 cup dry lentils or split peas

[1] Stretch out a balloon by blowing it up and
releasing the air.

[2] Using the funnel, pour lentils or split peas
into the balloon. Knot balloon securely and
cut off excess.

[3] Stretch out another balloon by blowing it up and releasing the air. Then cut the neck of the balloon off and stretch the remaining part over the lentil-stuffed balloon. Repeat with the third balloon.

[4] Hack till you have had it.

*Rules* There are only two rules: (1) The footbag can't touch the ground, and (2) you can't use your hands. Players kick and catch the bag only with their legs and feet, and the idea is to keep the bag off the ground as long as you can. It's like juggling with your feet, and it's harder than it sounds. It's also strangely addictive and is probably responsible for more skipped classes than any other sport.

*Variation*

**Make three sacks for juggling.**

# go fly
## a kite

*Windy days are bad for your coif but great for kite flying. Whip up this easy, breezy kite the next time there's a windy day and enjoy those gusts with gusto. This kite's not superstrong, though, so don't fly it when it's too windy, or it will take a one-way trip skyward.*

### You will need:

½ yard sail material (use rip-stop nylon fabric, heavy wrapping paper, or brightly colored butcher paper)

Scissors

Assorted decorating supplies: sequins, glitter, felt cutouts, rickrack trim, stickers, markers, or whatever you'd like

Strong tape (like packing tape, electrical tape, or duct tape)

2 dowels, each 12 inches

1 yard of string

3 pieces of ribbon, each 24 inches

Spool of kite thread

[1] Fold sail material in half and cut as illustrated in diagram A.

[2] Unfold material and decorate any way you like.

[3] Tape dowels securely to the back of your kite as shown in diagram B.

[4] Knot your piece of string to make a loop in the very middle. Then tie a double knot at each end of the string. Tape the ends of the string to the side corners of the kite to form a bridle as in diagram C.

[5] Tape your three pieces of ribbon to the bottom of the kite to make tails.

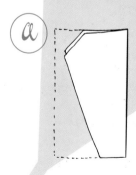

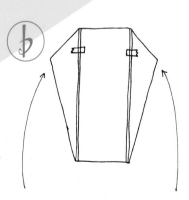

*continued on next page*

[6] Tie kite thread to the loop in the middle of bridle. Then tuck your 'do into a fetching headscarf and take this bad boy outside.

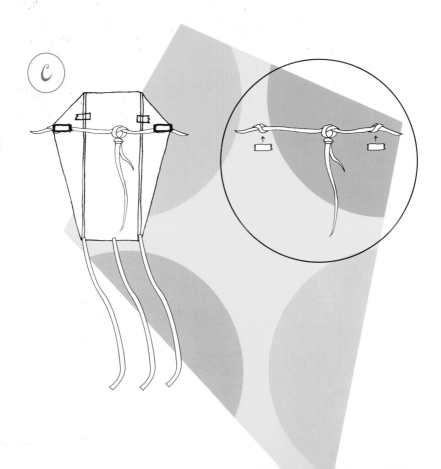

# seltzer
# sputnik

> Don't think you can turn Alka-Seltzer and a toilet paper tube into a jet-propelled spaceship? Of course you can! It ain't rocket science. Oh, wait—it is. Have an adult on hand to supervise. One small step for Crafty Girl, one giant step for Crafty Kind.

## You will need:

Masking tape

Cardboard tube from toilet paper roll

Paper plate

Construction paper, markers, glitter (optional)

Alka-Seltzer antacid tablet

Empty film canister (Fujifilm canisters are highly recommended. They are clear, so you can see your experiment in action, and they have very secure caps. If you don't have any around the house, you can get them for free from any photo-processing shop.)

Water

*continued on next page*

[1] Securely tape toilet paper tube to stand in center of paper plate. This forms your launch pad. If you like, you can decorate it with construction paper, markers, or glitter.

[2] Cut Alka-Seltzer tablet into quarters. Fill film canister half full with water.

[3] Take your launch pad, your Alka-Seltzer, and your film canister outside. Set up launch pad and get ready to work fast.

[4] Drop an Alka-Seltzer quarter into film canister. Quickly cap the canister and drop it upside down into toilet paper tube. Then stand back, and 3 … 2 … 1 … blastoff! Watch the Seltzer Sputnik fly! The Alka-Seltzer and water form carbon dioxide inside the canister, which blows off the cap and propels the canister. By varying the amount of water, the amount of Alka-Seltzer, and the angle of the toilet paper tube, you can make the canister fly faster and higher or farther.

# bubble
## brew

Bubble, bubble, no toil, no trouble. This bubble solution mixes up in seconds. Then go find yourself a hammock and blow the blues away.

### You will need:

1 cup water

2 tablespoons dishwashing liquid

1 tablespoon glycerin
(available at drugstores)

10-ounce bottle

Pipe cleaner

[ 1 ] Combine water, dishwashing liquid, and glycerin in your bottle. Cap tightly and shake well.

[ 2 ] Twist one end of your pipe cleaner into a loop to form a wand.

continued on next page

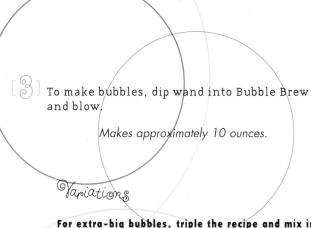

[3] To make bubbles, dip wand into Bubble Brew and blow.

*Makes approximately 10 ounces.*

## Variations

**For extra-big bubbles, triple the recipe and mix ingredients up in a big bowl or frying pan. Add a few extra squirts of dishwashing liquid. You can also add $\frac{1}{4}$ cup corn syrup for really huge bubbles, but if you do, you'll need to let the brew sit for a few hours before using it. When you're ready to blow, make a giant wand out of a coat hanger.**

# swimming pool
# *regatta*

*Now you can enjoy motorboat racing even if you're land-locked. A bottle and some baking soda will turn your swimming pool into a marine speedway. Have an adult on hand to supervise the jet propulsion action.*

## You will need:

2 tablespoons baking soda

2 squares of toilet paper

20-ounce plastic soda bottle, clean and dry, with cap

¼ cup vinegar

A swimming pool or a friend with a swimming pool

[ 1 ] Place 1 tablespoon of baking soda on each square of toilet paper. Fold paper so baking soda is enclosed inside. Place these packets inside your soda bottle.

*continued on next page*

[2] You'll have to do this next part really, really fast, so be ready. Pour vinegar into soda bottle and quickly cap bottle, twisting bottle cap only once so bubbles can escape. Place bottle in the pool and watch it go.

[3] If you like, you can race boats against each other, experimenting with different size bottles and different amounts of baking soda and vinegar. Award the winner the America's Cup. If you don't have one lying around the house, you could substitute a Reese's Cup instead.

# crafty
# scavenger hunt

*Sure, scavenger hunts are fun, but for a Crafty Girl like you, they're just not challenging enough. You need a Crafty Scavenger Hunt. Not only do you have to find things, you have to make things. The clock is ticking, your heart is racing, and you're flying through the neighborhood with a basket of freshly completed crafts under your arm. Who said crafting isn't a full-contact sport?*

### You will need:

Computer and printer OR pen, paper, and a photocopier

Crafty friends

Indulgent neighbors

A prize for the winning team

[1] First make up your Crafty Scavenger Hunt challenge list. Here are some ideas to get you started:

- Make a painting from condiments.
- Make a dress from a trash bag.
- Make a ring from a bag twist-tie.
- Make a frame from a cereal box.
- Make a purse from a margarine tub.

*continued on next page*

- Make spectacles from pipe cleaners.
- Make sandals from cardboard and string.
- Make a tiara from aluminum foil.
- Make a mask from a paper plate and string.
- Make a hat from an oatmeal canister.
- Make a dog-sized fez from a paper cup.
- Make a wig from yarn or cottonballs.
- Make a flower from a tissue.
- Make an anklet from flowers.
- Make a boat from a milk carton.
- Make a bug out of chewing gum (unchewed, please).
- Make a puppet from a plastic glove.
- Make a necklace from cereal and thread.
- Make a bracelet from candy wrappers.
- Make a lei from crepe paper.

Print or photocopy a copy of the list for each player.

[2] Now you're ready to play. Begin by splitting into teams. Give each player a copy of the challenge list, and you're on your way.

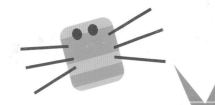

[3] Each team must gather all the materials and make all the crafts. You can conduct the hunt indoors or scour the neighborhood. Players can be fashioning their crafts while scavenging.

[4] When done, the team reports back to the starting point.

[5] The team that finishes first wins the prize and the undying admiration of the whole block.

part 2
rainy day doings

# light-as-a-feather
# foam glider

Paper airplanes are pretty fun, but let's face it: there are only so many variations on a theme. You make either a jet or a glider. It either soars or swoops. Whoopee.

Homemade planes don't have to be so dull, though. If you really want the fun to take off, vary your materials and your design. Add vents and cutaways. Try making a plane out of construction paper, craft foam, even aluminum foil. Make a Wonder Woman–style invisible plane out of a transparency sheet. Race your creations against each other to see what different variations do. If style counts as much as speed, decorate your plane with airline logos or flashy stickers, and if you want to get really fancy, tape several together to make them fly in formation. Don a flight attendant costume, pin wings to your lapel, and wheel a cart of refreshments around to spectators while the paper airshow is going on.

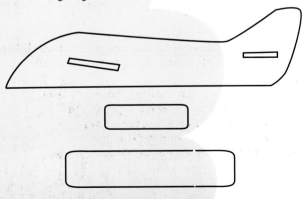

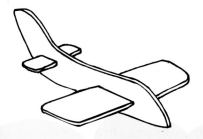

*Still yawning? This fluffy confection of a foam glider should get your jets going.*

## You will need:

Ballpoint pen

8-by-10-inch piece of craft foam (available at craft stores)

Scissors

White glue (optional)

Feathers for decoration (optional)

[1] Use a ballpoint pen to trace the shapes shown onto your craft foam. You'll probably want to make them bigger.

[2] Cut out the shapes you've just traced. Cut two slits as shown. Slide wings into slits.

[3] If you'd like, you can decorate your glider by gluing on feathers. It seems appropriate, given the project name. Besides, there's always a chance your cat will mistake your feathered flier for a bird, and wouldn't that be a hoot?

# soda bottle bowling

*Soda Bottle Bowling will put the fizz back in a day that's gone flat. Rummage through the recycling bin for supplies, and in no time you've transformed the hallway into your very own bowling lane.*

### You will need:

10 plastic soda bottles, each 1 liter, cleaned and dried

Assorted decorating supplies: paint, glitter, glue, beads, construction paper, stickers, or whatever you like (optional)

Funnel

10 cups rice, beans, or sand

Ball, 12 inches in circumference or so (you could also use a ball of yarn)

Paper and pen

 [ 1 ] Decorate your soda bottles any way you like. If you're a Lady of the Lanes, coat them with glitter and rhinestones. If you're a Bowling Betty, paint them with classic red stripes. Paint faces on them or affix stickers, ribbons, shapes you've cut from construction paper, or whatever you like. Allow everything to set and dry. Or skip the decorations altogether and get right to the action.

[2] Use a funnel to fill each bottle with 1 cup of rice, beans, or sand. Get your ball and take a couple test rolls. If the pins knock over too easily, add more rice. If they don't knock over easily enough, remove some rice.

[3] Set up your bottle bowling pins: five in the back row, then three, then two, then one pin in front.

4 With your paper and pen, make a score sheet, or photocopy and enlarge the one on the next page.

[5] Step back a few yards and you're ready to roll.

continued on next page

89

| NAME: | | | | | | | | | | |
|---|---|---|---|---|---|---|---|---|---|---|
| | | | | | | | | | | |
| | | | | | | | | | | |
| | | | | | | | | | | |

# Rules

Players take turns trying to knock down the pins. Each player gets to roll twice per turn. You get one point for each pin you knock down. If you knock all the pins down at once, that's a strike. If you knock them all down in two rolls, that's a spare. Either of these stupendous achievements is worthy of a special prize.

Official scoring is pretty tricky. If you are a bowling maven, it is worth learning all the rules regarding strikes and spares (you can use the official scoresheet above). But as a Crafty Girl, your time may be better spent making the world a fun and funky place. Feel free to skip the official league rules and make up your own (we do). Some Crafty Girls we know award a chocolate bar every time all ten pins are knocked down. Others reward gutter balls (balls that hit nothing) with sour candies. Play loud music and develop unusual bowling techniques. It's your thing—do what you want to do. At the end of the game, tally up everyone's points. Whoever has the highest score wins, and must celebrate by doing a funky lane dance.

# hallway

## croquet

*If Soda Bottle Bowling isn't quite sophisticated enough for you, perhaps you would enjoy a round of Hallway Croquet. Wickets without the weeds—how civilized. If there's a break in the clouds and the ground's not too wet, though, you can play outside, too.*

### You will need:

Scissors

1 or more frozen juice or lemonade containers, clean and dry, with end caps intact

1 or more yardsticks (same number as the juice containers)

Masking Tape

Assorted decorating supplies: tempera or acrylic craft paint, colored tape, construction paper, or whatever you'd like

11 pipe cleaners, each 12 inches long

Spangly gift wire (optional)

Fun-Tak wall-mount adhesive gum or 1-inch squares of craft foam

1 ball for each player, 5 inches in diameter or smaller (tennis balls or golf balls will work just fine)

Stickers in different colors

*continued on next page*

[ 1 ] Cut a slot in the middle of the juice container just big enough to insert the yardstick. Slide yardstick in and tape in place. Tape end caps in place, too. Now you have a croquet mallet. You do not, however, have a stylish croquet mallet, and style is very important in croquet. Decorate your mallet with paint, colored tape, construction-paper cutouts, or whatever you'd like. If you're good at sharing, you're done with mallet crafting. If not, you'll need to make another mallet for each player.

[ 2 ] Make nine wickets by bending nine of the pipe cleaners into horseshoe shapes big enough for the balls to pass through, twisting two pipe cleaners together if necessary. You can decorate the wickets by wrapping spangly gift wire around them. Next you'll need to help keep the wickets upright. You can use a little wad of Fun-Tak on each wicket end if you're playing on wood or tile floors. If you're playing on carpet, construct a little foot by taping a small square of craft foam to each end.

[ 3 ] Make two endposts by taking the remaining two pipe cleaners and attaching either Fun-Tak or foam feet.

[4] Mark each player's ball with a different-colored sticker so you'll be able to tell them all apart.

[5] Set up your croquet course by placing the wickets in a figure eight shape, with a wicket and an endpost at both the top and the bottom.

[6] Get dressed in your toniest whites, and you're ready to play.

Rules There are many versions of croquet, but we like the simplest one best. Play counterclockwise, going up the right side of the figure eight and down the left, getting one hit per turn plus one extra hit every time you go through a wicket or collide with another player's ball. If you get back to the starting endpost first, you win. Win extra points for looking super-stylish.

START/END

# supermodel
## stilts

> They say supermodels have to be tall. These stilts will give you an extra 6 inches fast. Then it's sashay. And turn. Stop. And pose. Work it, baby, work it!

### You will need:

2 coffee cans

Hammer and nail

Assorted decorating supplies: paint, glitter, glue, beads, rhinestones, construction paper, stickers, or whatever you'd like (optional)

2 lengths of pretty, narrow ribbon, each 6 feet

[ 1 ] Have an adult put two holes, at opposite sides, near the top of each coffee can, by hammering a nail through can. Remove the nail after the hole is created.

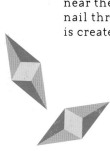

[2] Next you'll need to decorate the coffee cans. Think of your stilts as extreme platform shoes and embellish accordingly. Paint them with swirly, funky designs. Glue on cardboard cutouts and glitter, or cover the entire cans with beads and rhinestones.

[3] Make handles by threading ribbon into the holes. Knot ends securely inside the can, where the knot will be hidden from view.

[4] Climb aboard your Supermodel Stilts, pulling on the handles to keep the cans tight against your soles. Then strut down that catwalk, pretty lady.

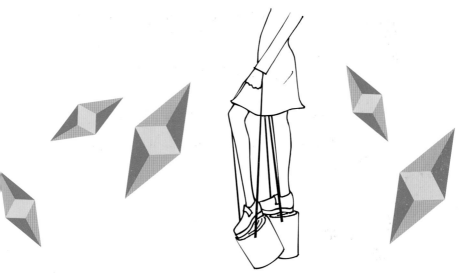

# fill in
## the blanks

*Fill in the Blanks are like Mad Libs gone completely insane. Take a passage from your favorite book, blank out the key words, and fill in the fun. Cut loose Crafty Girl–style and learn a little grammar while you do.*

### You will need:

Books, magazines, pamphlets, or other written material

A computer and printer

Construction paper

Stapler or brads

[1] First you'll need to find some funny passages to use. Flip through your favorite books and magazines. Skim pamphlets, papers, even cereal boxes. Peruse the yearbook, the school bulletin, or homework assignments. You never know what will provide great Fill in the Blank material. (The funniest one we ever did came from a biography of the New Kids on the Block. Go figure.) Find at least 10 good passages, each one paragraph long.

[2] Type up your passages on the computer. Then go back and delete some words, replacing each with an apt description or naming the part of speech, in caps. So if you delete "Shakespeare," you'll replace it with "FAMOUS WRITER." If you delete "write," you'll replace it with "VERB." If you delete "Alas!" you'll replace it with "EXCLAMATION." And so on. Delete at least 10 words per passage and be sure to leave a blank space before each description, so you can write something in later.

[3] Print out your passages. Make a pretty cover from construction paper and bind the whole thing together with staples or brads.

[4] To play, ask your friends to name a FAMOUS WRITER, a VERB, an EXCLAMATION—whatever the descriptive capitals call for. Write down their suggestions in the blanks, then read the whole passage aloud. "EDGAR ALLAN POE dressed himself in his favorite DISCO HOT PANTS. He was eager to go ROLLER-SKATE. On his way, he noticed his chambermaid had DROOLED upon his master-piece. 'DON'T GO THERE, GIRL!' he exclaimed." Bah hah hah hah hah.

# flipbooks

Before The Simpsons, before The Flintstones, there were flipbooks. Flipbooks use Stone Age animation technology to make simple cartoons at home. It won't be a Disney masterpiece, but you can easily illustrate a person running, a plant growing, or a flower losing its petals.

## You will need:

Scissors

3 sheets of white paper, each 8½ by 11 inches

Stapler

Pen or pencil

[1] Cut each sheet of white paper into eighths, making 24 rectangles total. Staple all of the rectangles together to make a little book.

[2] Draw a figure on the first page. Keep it simple, because you'll have to draw the same basic figure 23 more times. A stick person or stick animal or a simple plant or flower would work well.

[3] On the next page, draw the same figure, only slightly moved. If it's a person running, draw the arms and legs a little higher. If it's a plant, draw it slightly bigger. If it's a flower, draw it with one less petal. Repeat 22 more times, moving the figure slightly each time. It's easiest to work from back to front, so you can trace the figure underneath, varying it just a bit.

49

[4] When you're all done, flip through the book quickly and see your picture in action.

# twist and shout

*You love having an excuse to (gently) plant an elbow in your brother's nose, and now you do. Play a round of Twist and Shout! Whose knee is in my back?*

**You will need:**

2 pieces of white construction paper, each 8½ by 11 inches, cut into eighths

Markers

2 bowls

6 pieces of green construction paper

6 pieces of red construction paper

6 pieces of yellow construction paper

6 pieces of blue construction paper

red

[1] Get your 16 little pieces of white construction paper. Write "red," "yellow," "green," and "blue" on 4 of them and place them in a bowl. On the remaining 12 slips, write the names of body parts. You'll want right foot, left foot, right hand, left hand, of course, but you should get as crazy and creative as you want to be. Right ear! Belly button! Big left toe! Right funny bone! Put these 12 slips in the other bowl.

*yellow*

[2] Scatter the sheets of colored construction paper on the floor. You want them close enough so it will be possible to reach red with your left pinky while you've got your right knee on blue, but not so close that it will be easy.

[3] Designate a caller, and you're ready to play. The caller will pick 1 slip from the body part bowl and 1 slip from the color bowl and read them aloud together: "Nose on yellow!" All players must then press their noses to a yellow square. Then the caller returns the slips to the appropriate bowls, picks 1 from each again, and so on and so on.

[4] Once you've got a body part on a square, it has to stay stuck there. If you unstick yourself, slip, fall, foam at the mouth, bite or lick another player, or make a face that makes a child cry, you're disqualified. The player who lasts the longest in the game wins.

*blue*

*green*

# autobiographical
# board games

You've got some free time, a piece of posterboard, and dice. Why not make a board game? You could design a Monopoly-type game based on your block or your school. You could make a game about your favorite hobby, be it soccer or sandwiches. It could be more personal, for instance being called "Get to Know Me," where players could advance only by answering questions about you. Or by paying you compliments. It's your game: you get to make up the rules, and if one of the rules is that other players have to bring you bonbons, then so be it. Here are some ideas for a basic board game to adapt any way you like.

## You will need:

Markers

16-by-20-inch piece of posterboard (or borrow a board from a game you already have)

Assorted decorating supplies: stickers, glitter, paint, pictures, or whatever you'd like

20 pieces of cardstock, each 2 by 3 inches

8½-by-11-inch piece of paper

Dice

skip a turn!

chocolate you can until your next turn

[ 1 ] Draw your game board onto the posterboard. The game should consist of consecutive squares (you'll want at least 30) that can be strung together in any shape you like: a square, a snake, a figure eight, an ice cream cone, or your profile. Decorate with stickers, glitter, paint, pictures, or whatever you'd like. Otherwise, just borrow a board from a game you already have.

[ 2 ] Write directions on the squares, like "Skip a turn," "Roll again," etc. If you're using a board borrowed from a store-bought game, just write your directions on blank Post-its and stick them to the existing squares. Get as creative as you'd like. Some examples:
- "Wear a shower cap until you roll a six."
- "Go back 2 squares and suck a lemon for 5 minutes."
- "Eat all the chocolate you can until your next turn."
- "Do the Hokey-Pokey until you roll a four."
- "Wear your socks on your hands until someone else rolls a two."
- "Advance 3 squares and pay the hostess a compliment."
- "Pretend you're the age of the number you just rolled until your next turn."

On several squares, write, "Take a Question Card."

continued on next page

Next, make your Question Cards by writing a question on each piece of cardstock. If your game is all about you, your questions might include the following:

- "What is my most appealing quality?"
- "Which beautiful superstar do I most resemble?"
- "When is my birthday, and what present do you plan to give me?"
- "Which adjective describes me best: 'sparkling,' 'bubbly,' or 'radiant'?"

At the bottom of each card, add a reward and a penalty for getting the answer right or wrong. Some examples:

- "Advance 2 squares for answering correctly; go back 2 and moo like a cow for answering incorrectly."
- "Advance 1 square and pet the cat for answering correctly; go back 1 and pet the lizard for answering incorrectly."
- "Advance to the kitchen and fetch me a lemonade with lots of ice, as neither a right nor a wrong answer is any help in quenching my thirst."

Then make your answer key on the 8½-by-11-inch piece of paper. Entrust the answer key to someone who's not playing the game, and have him or her verify right or wrong answers when question cards are drawn.

[4] Play by rolling dice and following the directions on each square as you land on them. The player who gets to the end first wins—unless, of course, one of the rules is that you win every time no matter what.

What is my most appealing quality?

Which beautiful superstar do I most resemble?

# custom

## car~bingo

Your family's road trips are rituals. Every time you're all in a car for more than an hour, your brother keeps asking if you're there yet, Dad spills hot coffee in his lap, the dog barks at pickup trucks, and Mom sings loudly and off-key.

Now you can turn everyone's annoying habits into a game. Assemble Custom Car-Bingo boards and have everyone play along. You'll be at Grandma's house before you know it.

### You will need:

Pen

4 pieces of paper, each 8½ by 11 inches

4 pieces of cardboard, each 8½ by 11 inches

4 transparency sheets (available at office-supply stores), each 8½ by 11 inches

8 binder clips

4 dry-erase markers

[ 1 ] Draw a grid 5 squares by 5 squares in the middle of each piece of paper. The squares should be large enough to write in, about 1 inch square.

[2] Write "FREE" in the center squares. In the rest
of the squares, write things you normally see,
hear, smell, or experience on car trips with
your family, like:

- Rover drools out the window.
- Dad threatens to turn the car around.
- We are overwhelmed by fumes from
  the cattle farm.
- Caitlin gets gum stuck in her hair.
- Caitlin gets gum stuck in Rover's hair.
- Mom makes us listen to a really
  lame radio station.
- A kid in another car sticks his
  tongue out at us.
- Josh asks to make a pit stop.
- Dad asks, "Why didn't you take care of
  that before we left the house?"
- We get pulled over for speeding.
- Josh and Caitlin fight over the GameBoy.
- Mom and Dad cave in to whining and
  let us stop for fast-food.

Make each of the four grids different.

[3] Assemble bingo boards as follows: place each
gridded piece of paper on a piece of cardboard.
Top each with a transparency sheet. Secure
each board with two binder clips.

[4] To play, check off squares on the transparency
sheet as you see or experience the events
described. The first person to check off a horizon-
tal, vertical, or diagonal line 5 squares long wins.

# the indoor snack farm

## experiment

Don't get too excited. We're not talking about growing potato chips or cupcakes, but if you're lucky and patient, you can grow popcorn, garlic, beans, and carrots. Healthy, sure, but tasty, too.

**You will need:**

1 paper cup for each plant

½ cup soil for each plant

Things to plant: popcorn kernels, garlic cloves, apple seeds, beans, leafy carrot tops, etc.

Labels

Pen

[1] Fill each paper cup with ½ cup soil.

[2] Plant a seed or cutting in each cup, about 2 inches down in the soil. Experiment. Get creative. Try planting sunflower seeds or soybeans, garlic cloves, popcorn kernels, or anything you think might sprout. (Don't even *try* planting potato chips or cupcakes. It ain't gonna happen.) Record what you've planted on a label and stick label on cup.

[3] Place your cups in a nice, sunny place. Water often enough to keep soil a little damp. Check your plants every day. What sprouts first? What grows fastest? What doesn't grow at all? If it turns out your thumb is not so much green as the black digit of death, start again with a new batch of potential plants.

# fantasy

 fort

> *Sofa cushions and blankets were fine when you were younger, but now you want a more sophisticated fort. This one looks like the inside of a genie's bottle. So fold your arms, blink, nod, and work that ponytail. Your Fantasy Fort wish is our command.*

## You will need:

5-foot length of PVC tubing, 2 to 3 inches in diameter (available at hardware stores), OR a 5-foot pole, OR, failing all else, 2 cardboard tubes from wrapping paper rolls (the sturdier, the better), each 30 inches long, taped securely together end to end (5-foot total length)

Wrapping paper

Clear tape

Dinner plate

Duct tape

Pretty rocks or crystals

4 pretty color-coordinated sheets, queen size or larger

Needle and thread OR 50 safety pins

Throw pillows

Scarves

Flashlights

Small tape player or CD player and
belly dance music

Refreshments

[1] Your PVC tubing, pole, or cardboard will form a tent
pole, but before it does, you need to gussy it up. Wrap
it in some pretty wrapping paper and secure with
clear tape.

[2] Next you'll need to construct a base to keep
your tent pole upright. Stand the pole on top
of a dinner plate. Make sure it's straight, then
secure in place with lots and lots of duct tape.
Conceal the tape by spreading pretty rocks or
crystals around the plate (this will also help
anchor the tent pole in place).

[3] Now you'll make the top by joining your four sheets
together to form one giant square. You can baste
them together with needle and thread or, if you're
a clumsy seamstress, just safety-pin them together
as artfully as you can. Drape the giant sheet square
over the tent pole to make a teepee.

*continued on next page*

[4] Work your interior decorating magic. Strew throw pillows and pretty scarves on the floor. Light your fort with flashlights placed near the tent pole. Do not use candles (we know: they're so pretty—but so dangerous, so ix-nay on the andles-cay).

[5] An important part of genie tradition is hospitality, so invite Aladdin, Jasmine, and the rest of your friends over. Entertain them with belly dance music and serve meze platters of snacks, like hummus and pita and halvah and peach juice. You're rocking the Casbah, all right.

# fortune-telling
## fun

*Once you've got your Fantasy Fort established, why not set up shop as a fortune-teller? There are many methods of fortune-telling: horoscopes, tarot cards, crystal balls, cootie catchers, divination pendulums, and palm-reading. We prefer fortune cookies and tea leaves, because they predict the future and provide a tasty snack. Make a batch of the delicious Funny Fortune Cookies on page 117 to hand out to fort visitors with tea. Read the Oracle Board while they nosh. We see crafty fun in your future.*

## Tasseomancy Tea

### You will need:

1 cup water

1 tablespoon loose tea leaves

A simple, light-colored cup

[1] With adult supervision, bring water to a boil. While the water is bubbling, dump the tea leaves into your empty cup.

[2] Pour boiling water over tea leaves. Allow to steep and cool for 5 minutes or so. When the tea is cool enough, drink up. Savor. Relax.

continued on next page

[3] When there's only a teaspoon or two of tea left, swirl the tea around while concentrating on something in the future you're curious about. When the leaves settle down, look in your cup. What you see is your fortune. If you were wondering what you would get for your birthday and you see a pony shape in the tea leaves, you're a very fortunate girl.

*Makes 1 cup.*

## Oracle Board

**You will need:**

Markers

12-by-12-inch piece of posterboard

Assorted decorating supplies: stickers, glitter, rhinestones, glue, paint, or whatever you'd like

Single die

[1] Draw a grid on your posterboard, 4 squares by 4 squares, for a total of 16 squares.

[2] In each square write a different category and six choices. Some examples:

| PET | CITY | # OF KIDS | JOB |
|---|---|---|---|
| 1. Horse | 1. Honolulu | 1. 12 | 1. Car mechanic |
| 2. Iguana | 2. Peoria | 2. 3 | 2. Ice cream taster |
| 3. Platypus | 3. Cairo | 3. 0 | 3. Marine biologist |
| 4. Hairless cat | 4. St. Petersburg | 4. 6 | 4. Secretary of state |
| 5. Tarantula | 5. Hong Kong | 5. 2 | 5. Fish psychologist |
| 6. Teacup poodle | 6. Juneau | 6. 38 | 6. CIA operative |

[3] Decorate your board with glitter, rhinestones, stickers, or whatever you'd like.

[4] To play, roll a die onto the board grid. The die predicts the choice for whatever square it lands on. So, if your die ends up on the PET square and you have rolled a five, this means you'll be the proud owner of a tarantula. Lucky you.

pet city kids job

# part 3

## spy supplies and mad scientist materials

# cryptology
## crafts

*Passing notes is an art, indeed a craft. A Crafty Girl like you won't settle for ragged three-hole, ruled paper and chicken scratch. Your notes are masterpieces. More importantly, they are snoop-proof, artfully concealing their secrets. These projects will ensure your notes say nothing if they fall into the wrong hands.*

## Swiss Cheese Decoder Key

*A Swiss Cheese Decoder Key makes sense of a scrambled letter. Give one to your most trusted confidant.*

### You will need:

Small, pointy scissors, such as manicure or embroidery scissors

2 or more pieces of paper, each 8½ by 11 inches

Paper clips (optional)

Pen

[ 1 ] Using your small scissors, cut 30 or so word-sized holes (about 1 inch long by ¼ inch high) all over a page. When you're done, the page should look like Swiss cheese. If you have partners in crime, you'll want to make identical decoders, one for each of you. It's easiest to place two or more sheets together, secure with paper clips so they stay precisely aligned, and cut your message holes through both at once. Use them over and over. They'll never get the goods on you, shady lady.

[ 2 ] To use, place this Swiss Cheese Decoder over the blank piece of paper and write your message through the holes. Remove the decoder and write random words all over the rest of the message page. Your letter will look like nonsense by itself, but when you place the decoder over it, the message emerges.

## Invisible Ink

*Do we have to spell it out for you? If you have top secret information to pass on, you need invisible ink.*

### You will need:

8½-by-11-inch piece of paper

Toothpick

2 tablespoons lemon juice

Iron

*continued on next page*

[ 1 ] Tear the edges of your paper to give it an old, parchmenty look.

[ 2 ] Write your message on your paper, using a toothpick dipped in lemon juice as pen and ink. Don't use too much, or the paper will warp. When it dries, your message will be invisible.

[ 3 ] To read your letter, run an iron over the paper. Remember: paper + hot iron = fire, so don't leave the iron on long enough to singe, and do make sure an adult is present. The heat will make the writing appear.

## Jigsaw Letter

*As a covert operator, you're hard to read, and your letters are, too. This letter reveals itself when the recipient solves the puzzle.*

### You will need:

Marker

8-by-10-inch piece of posterboard

Pencil

Scissors

Envelope

1 Write your message in marker on the posterboard.

2 In pencil, draw interlocking, puzzle-shaped pieces all over the posterboard.

3 Cut out pieces along pencil lines.

4 Put pieces into an envelope and send to a trusted confidant. For extra security send the pieces in several different envelopes.

*Variation*

**A picture says a thousand words. Instead of writing a letter, you could glue a color copy of a photo to the posterboard, then cut into puzzle pieces.**

# counterintelligence

## booby traps

*Fifty percent of good spywork is defense. You're privy to highly sensitive, top secret information. You need to protect your findings by booby-trapping your room. Be sure to remember the traps are there, though, so you don't end up trapping yourself.*

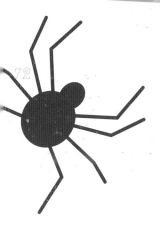

### You will need:

Construction paper

Markers

Honey

Transparent tape

Fake spiderwebbing, or white glue and wax paper

Plastic bugs, worms, snakes, or spiders

Sparkle Slime (recipe on page 76)

Hair

[1] Your first line of defense is a warning sign. Use the construction paper and marker to make a sign that will discourage intruders (a) by making them think that whatever's inside your room is incredibly boring or (b) making them think whatever's inside your room is incredibly dangerous or disgusting. Recommended signs: "Broom Closet. Authorized Personnel Only." "Snake Venom Milking Center. KEEP OUT." "Hassenpfeffer Limburger Cheese Factory. Smell Us Grow!"

[2] Next you'll want to booby-trap the door itself. You'll do this two ways. First, you'll dab a smidgen of honey on the doorknob, forcing intruders to go wash up rather than come on in (but don't forget it's there when *you* want to enter). Then you'll put a piece of transparent tape between the door and door frame in an inconspicuous place. If the tape is torn, you'll know an intruder was there.

[3] Your next line of defense is the gross-out factor. Festoon your entryway with fake spiderwebs; plastic bugs, worms, snakes, or spiders; and blobs of Sparkle Slime. Use store-bought spider webbing (easy to find at Halloween). Otherwise, make your own by drawing a spiderweb in white glue on wax paper; allow to dry, then peel off the glue web and hang wherever you want it.

[4] Finally, you'll want to booby-trap your most top secret possessions. Place a hair over your diary or any other secret treasure you may have. If the hair has moved when you return, you'll know someone was getting into your things.

# smuggler's
# rocks

*These creations look like ordinary rocks, but they hold treasures inside. They're a great way to smuggle your favorite little trinkets.*

## You will need:

1 cup flour

1 cup used coffee grounds

¼ cup salt

3 tablespoons sand or cornmeal

1 tablespoon oatmeal

1 cup water

Treasures to hide (anything small and unbreakable will do: tiny plastic toys, figurines, or rings all work well)

[1] Mix flour, coffee, salt, sand or cornmeal, oatmeal, and water together to form a dough. Transfer to a floured surface and knead until smooth and well mixed.

[2] Break dough into rock-sized pieces. Hide a treasure in the center of each piece. Don't hide anything really valuable—it will get rock grit all over it, and it might break when you later crack open the hardened rock. Not a good way to store the family jewels.

[3] Allow Smuggler's Rocks to dry for 4 days.

[4] When it's time to retrieve the treasure, carefully break rock on concrete.

*Makes 12 to 15 rocks.*

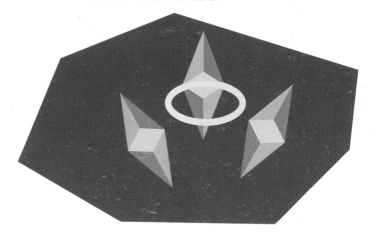

# sparkle
## slime

> Is it an outer space life form? Toxic waste? Drain sludge? No! It's the Creature That Came from Crafty Girl! Eeek! Ewww! Uggggh! It's so disgusting, we'd be surprised if you wanted to put it in your mouth, but we'll warn you, anyway: it ain't edible. You'll want to wash the stuff off your hands when you're done playing with it, too.

### You will need:

1½ teaspoons Borax (find it with the laundry supplies in the supermarket)

¾ cup water

¼ cup glue

Resealable plastic sandwich bag

Food coloring (green for swamp slime, blue for space slime, red for horror slime, yellow and green for radioactive slime)

2 teaspoons glitter (optional)

1 Dissolve Borax in just ½ cup water.

[2] In another cup mix together remaining ¼ cup water and glue. Stir well.

[3] Pour Borax mixture and glue mixture into your plastic bag. Add a few drops of food coloring and glitter, if using. Seal the bag. Knead the mixture, with bag still sealed, until everything's blended and congealed. Then open the bag and dig in.

[4] Store Sparkle Slime in the refrigerator when you're not using it. It will stay fresh for 2 weeks or so.

*Makes 1 cup.*

Uses

You can knead it, squish it, and squash it. You can fling it, but if you're planning to let the flubber fly, be warned: it will stain whatever it lands on. You can booby-trap your treasures by placing blobs of slime on plastic wrap as a deterrent. You can smear it on your locker to keep out intruders. You can dab it on yourself to make a fake wound or infection (but keep it far, far away from your eyes, mouth, and nose). You can tell gullible friends it's kryptonite. Sparkle Slime's uses are many, and more uses are invented every day. Slip a little resealable bag of the stuff in your backpack, and you will be the envy of all.

# shape-shifting
## ooey-goo

> It's a solid. It's a liquid. It's a solid. It's a liquid. It's Shape-Shifting Ooey-Goo. This is one of the easiest goos to make. It's also the messiest, so keep it in the kitchen and wear an apron. When you're finished, throw the goo in the garbage—not down the sink where it will gunk up the pipes.

**You will need:**

¼ cup cornstarch plus more as needed

¼ cup water plus more as needed

Food coloring (optional)

[1] Dump cornstarch into a bowl. Add water and a few drops of food coloring, if using. Mix with your fingers.

[2] Your goo should look like icing. If you've got a thick, crumbly paste instead, add more water, drop by drop. If you've got milky water, add a little more cornstarch, pinch by pinch. When it's the right consistency, you should be able to form a solid ball of dough between your palms.

[3] Then let the ball stretch out into disgusting, wet, gooey strings. Dough ball. Gooey strings. Dough ball. Gooey strings. Watch it shift back and forth until the thrill is gone.

*Makes ½ cup.*

# nutty
## putty

Nutty Putty is a big wad of moldable fun. Make a fake nose or Mr. Spock ears. Make imprints of your fingertips or toes. (Don't go making molds of your teeth, however: it's not edible. Besides, after a while who knows where it's been?) Nutty Putty will also pick up pigment, so you can spread it over comic strips and transfer the pictures onto it. When the putty's filthy, throw it out and mix up a new batch.

**You will need:**

½ cup white glue

½ cup liquid laundry starch

Food coloring (optional)

[1] Mix glue, starch, and a few drops of food coloring, if using, in a bowl. Stir until well blended.

[2] Allow to sit for 5 minutes.

[3] Stick your fingers in the blobby mixture. (Gross, we know—but fun!) Knead until it's the texture of Silly Putty. Don't give up if it takes a little while; it'll come together.

*Makes 1 cup.*

part 4

color chemistry

# sidewalk
## chalk

*There's nothing on TV. All your friends are off visiting their grandparents. It must be Sunday afternoon.*

*Despair no more. The answer to the Sunday afternoon doldrums is in the trash. You heard us: go get the shells from the eggs you had for brunch and turn them into chalk. Then, instead of watching the paint dry, you can paint the pavement. Sundays rock.*

### You will need:

Shells of 6 eggs, washed and dried

1 teaspoon flour

1 teaspoon hot water

Food coloring

Paper towel

[1] Grind your eggshells into a fine powder. If you have a mortar and pestle, this will be easy. If you don't, you can use a small metal bowl and a clean, smooth rock.

[2] Add flour, hot water, and a few drops of food coloring to eggshell powder. Mix until it forms a paste.

[3] Form mixture into a chalk stick. Roll stick in a strip of paper towel and allow to dry for 3 days.

[4] When chalk is dry, peel off paper towel, take it outside, and show the neighborhood you're a pavement Picasso.

*Makes 1 piece of chalk.*

## Variation

**You can also make chalk from plaster of Paris. Mix 1 cup plaster of Paris, 1 cup water, and food coloring. Allow to stand for a few minutes. Then pour into a small paper cup or a cardboard toilet paper tube. Allow to dry for a few days. When fully dry, peel away paper cup or toilet paper tube.**

# whirlwind
# watercolors

Vinegar, soda, and cornstarch may smell pretty bad, but
they turn into something beautiful: watercolors you tint
yourself. Mix up a batch and paint a dreamy masterpiece.

## You will need:

1 tablespoon white vinegar

2 tablespoons baking soda

1 tablespoon cornstarch

½ teaspoon glycerin (available at
drugstores)

½ teaspoon glitter (optional)

Muffin tin

Food coloring (food coloring paste,
available at baking-supply stores,
works best)

[ 1 ] Mix vinegar and baking soda in a bowl. It will
fizz and foam. When it stops foaming, add
cornstarch and glycerin and stir well. If you
want glitter watercolors, add the glitter now.

[2] Separate the mixture into muffin tin compartments.

[3] Add a different food coloring to each muffin compartment and stir in well. You'll want to use a lot. You can blend colors to get new shades. You already know how to make orange (1 part red to 1 part yellow), purple (1 part blue to 1 part red), and green (1 part blue to 1 part yellow). To make brown, use 1 part blue, 1 part red, and 2 parts yellow. Experiment with other combinations!

[4] Allow colors to dry overnight.

*Makes 1 set of paints.*

Note   When you're ready to begin your masterpiece, get a cup of water, and use your brush to moisten paint.

# fast-food
## finger paints

*This paint is the art equivalent of fast-food: quick, easy, and messy. Use it for finger painting or store it in mustard or ketchup bottles and squeeze out a modern art masterpiece.*

### You will need:

¼ cup flour

⅓ cup cold water

1 cup boiling water

¼ cup salt

Small Tupperware containers or squeeze bottles (dry, clean mustard or glue bottles work well)

Food coloring (food coloring paste, available at baking supply stores, works best)

[1] Combine flour and cold water in a bowl. Mix well. Then stir in boiling water. Add salt. Mix all this together.

[2] Portion mixture into small Tupperware containers or squeeze bottles.

**[3]** Add different food coloring to each.

**[4]** Allow paint to cool to room temperature. Then paint your *pièce de résistance*. If you're using squeeze bottles, experiment with Jackson Pollock-style abstract squiggles. You are a brilliant artiste, *n'est pas?*

*Makes about 2 cups.*

mustard

orange soda

pink lemonade

ketchup

purple cow

special sauce

boysenberry

blueberry pie

frosty

lettuce

pickle

relish

# Play clay

Play Clay is Play-Doh you can make at home. The best part: You get to customize it. You can make it fruit scented or glittery. You can make it any color you like. You've always thought there should be minty, gray Play-Doh, and now there can be. Have an adult supervise the cooking. Then go nuts.

## You will need:

2 cups flour

1 cup salt

4 teaspoons cream of tartar

2 cups water

2½ tablespoons vegetable oil

Food coloring (food coloring paste, available in cake-decorating stores, works best)

3 tablespoons glitter (optional)

2 teaspoons vanilla, lemon, or mint extract (optional)

[1] In a pan combine flour, salt, and cream of tartar. Mix well, then add water and oil. Blend until mixture is smooth.

[2] Cook mixture over medium heat until a big ball of dough forms. Remove from heat.

[3] When dough cools, knead in food coloring and, if using, glitter. If you want scented dough, knead in flavor extract, too.

[4] Store Play Clay in an airtight container or resealable plastic bag. It will remain pliable for several weeks. If you want to keep a Play Clay figurine forever, allow it to air-dry for a few days.

*Makes about 5 cups.*

# special effects
## face paint

*Sometimes you want to look more gory than gorgeous. Maybe you're putting on a creature feature or making a monster movie. These concoctions will help you look the part.*

## Fake Blood

### You will need:

¼ cup corn syrup

½ teaspoon red food coloring

Blue food coloring (optional)

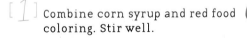 [ 1 ] Combine corn syrup and red food coloring. Stir well.

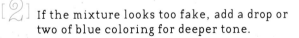 [ 2 ] If the mixture looks too fake, add a drop or two of blue coloring for deeper tone.

[ 3 ] Apply wherever you need a fake boo-boo. Keep it away from clothes, carpets, and furniture, though—it will stain whatever it touches.

*Makes ¼ cup*

# Scar Makeup

## You will need:

1 package gelatin (use unflavored for plain scars, cherry for bloody scars, lemon for infected scars—gross!—lime for monster scars, blue raspberry for alien scars)

2 tablespoons hot (not boiling) tap water

Cornstarch or baby powder (optional)

Liquid foundation (optional)

Black or gray eye shadow (optional)

Grape-nuts cereal or cooked rice (optional)

[ 1 ] Mix gelatin and water in a bowl and stir until the mixture thickens.

[ 2 ] As soon as it's cool enough, quickly apply scar tissue wherever you want it.

[ 3 ] If you like, you can dust scar tissue with cornstarch or baby powder for a more realistic effect (this works especially well on unflavored gelatin). You can also highlight the raised part of the scar tissue with liquid foundation and shade the contours with black or gray eye shadow.

[ 4 ] For a final, disgusting touch, you can sprinkle foreign matter in the scar tissue. Grape-nuts make realistic-looking gravel (color Grape-nuts black for even more realism). Grains of cooked rice look like maggots. You're sick, you know that?

*Makes about 2 tablespoons.*

# crystal
## garden

It would truly be a wonderful world if rubies, emeralds, sapphires, and diamonds grew on trees. They don't, but pretty crystals can grow on charcoal briquettes, and that's sort of a consolation, isn't it? Have an adult supervise the proceedings—the crystals require some chemical crafting.

### You will need:

4 charcoal briquettes

Glass pie plate

Spray bottle filled with water

¼ cup water

¼ cup laundry bluing (available in the laundry aisle of the supermarket)

¼ cup salt (plain, NOT iodized)

1 tablespoon ammonia

Food coloring

 [ 1 ] Break the charcoal into pieces approximately 1 inch square. The easiest way to do this is probably to pound them on concrete, but do whatever works for you. Place the pieces in a glass pie plate and spray them with water until they're good and soaked.

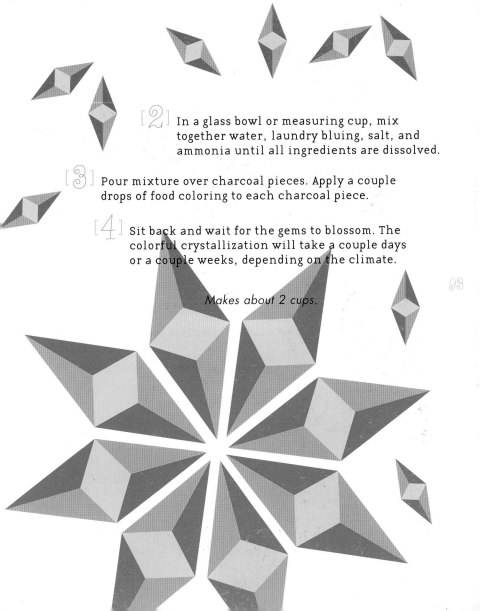

[2] In a glass bowl or measuring cup, mix together water, laundry bluing, salt, and ammonia until all ingredients are dissolved.

[3] Pour mixture over charcoal pieces. Apply a couple drops of food coloring to each charcoal piece.

[4] Sit back and wait for the gems to blossom. The colorful crystallization will take a couple days or a couple weeks, depending on the climate.

*Makes about 2 cups.*

# puffy
## paint

> Why should paint be flat? This 3-D paint will add a new dimension to your artwork. The salt crystals make it sparkly.

## You will need:

½ cup flour

½ cup salt

½ cup water

Food coloring (food coloring paste, available at baking-supply stores, works best)

Squeeze bottle (a dry, clean mustard or glue bottle will work well)

Construction paper

[1] Combine flour, salt, and water in a bowl. Mix well. Stir in food coloring.

[2] Transfer mixture to your squeeze bottle.

[3] To apply, simply squeeze out a design onto construction paper. When the paint dries, it will be puffy and sparkly.

*Makes 1½ cups.*

# confetti
## kaleidoscope

Confetti and Pringles are the ingredients for a pretty good party. They're also the ingredients for the easy, snazzy Confetti Kaleidoscope. Watch the pretty colors. Enjoy the faint aroma of potatoes. Now that's a good time.

## You will need:

Clean, empty cylindrical Pringles potato chip container

Plastic wrap

Sturdy tape

1 teaspoon confetti, sequins, or novelty glitter shapes

3 mirrors, each 2⅛-by-9-inches (Any glass store should be happy to cut these to order for you. If that seems like too much of a production, you can just wrap 3 pieces of 2⅛-by-9-inch light cardboard in aluminum foil, but be warned: the end result won't be nearly as cool.)

Ballpoint pen

Circle of construction paper roughly 4 inches in diameter

Pretty wrapping paper

continued on next page

[1] Pry the metal bottom off your Pringles container. A bottle opener will make the job easier. An adult with strong forearms will make the job a breeze.

[2] Remove the plastic cap from the Pringles container and set aside. Stretch a piece of plastic wrap over the top and tape securely in place on the sides. Sprinkle confetti, sequins, or glitter into the plastic cap you just set aside. Flip container and pop confetti-filled cap on the end covered with plastic wrap (see diagram A).

[3] Tape mirrors securely together, reflective sides facing in, to form a triangular tube the length of the Pringles container. You should end up with something shaped like a large Toblerone bar. Slide this unit into the container (see diagram B).

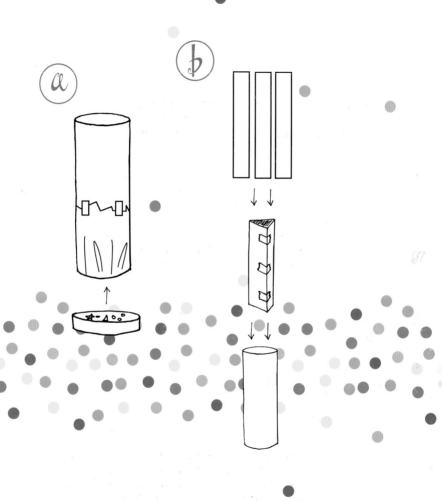

continued on next page

[4] Use the ballpoint pen to punch a pea-sized hole in the center of your construction paper. Place construction paper over the open end of the Pringles container and tape securely in place. Use lots and lots of sturdy tape and good, heavy construction paper—you don't want the mirrors sliding out and bonking you.

[5] Cover the sides of the Pringles container in pretty wrapping paper.

[6] Then look through the pea-sized hole and check out the psychedelic fractals. Ooh. Ahh.

# cultured

## coloring books

*You're mature. Sophisticated. You still enjoy the occasional coloring book, but you're looking for an activity that's more challenging than just staying in the lines. Here are some ideas to make coloring books a little more cultured.*

### Posh Pointillism

*We suspect this is how the young Seurat colored in his coloring books.*

**You will need:**

Coloring book

Markers (you'll need a lot of different colors—one of those 50-pen sets is best)

Ornate frame

[1] There's not much to it: simply color in the page with tiny dots instead of strokes. Use lots of different colors to get variations in shade. If you're coloring an apple, you'll color the darker parts with dots of red, black, gray, and brown. The lighter parts will call for dots of red, pink, and tan. You get the idea.

*continued on next page*

[2] To admire your work, step back a few feet.
See how the picture emerges from the dots?

[3] When you're done, place your artwork in
the ornate frame it deserves.

## Au Courant Cubism

*A coloring book tribute to Picasso.*

### You will need:

Coloring book

Pastels

Frame

[1] We command you to color outside the lines. Convey
the *sense* of the picture with angles, lines, geometric
shapes. That apple becomes a big, juicy trapezoid.

[2] Place your picture in a frame, then step
back and check it out. When it comes to
coloring, baby, you're no square.

# Mosaic Moderne

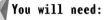

*You don't have to color with pens, paints, or pastels. Why not use beads or sequins instead? If you're really crafty, or really hungry, use candy. Strands of licorice become hair, jellybeans become eyes. Give new meaning to "artistic taste."*

### You will need:

Coloring book

White glue

Beads, sequins, or candy (Seed beads work best, because they are small enough to depict details as tiny as eyelashes. Be warned, however, that the smaller the bead, the slower the going. It takes about 40 hours to cover an entire page with seed beads.)

Toothpick (optional)

Sponge brush

Glossy, clear acrylic sealer

Frame

[1] Fill in the picture by gluing down beads, sequins, candy, or anything else you can think of. It's generally easiest to apply glue to a small area of the page, then apply the beads. A toothpick makes the application easier.

[2] After your mosaic is completed and the glue is set, use your sponge brush to give the work a good coating of glossy, clear acrylic sealer. Be careful not to dislodge any beads.

[3] Allow the acrylic sealer to dry. Then place your fabulous coloring creation in a worthy frame.

**part 5**

# kitchen chaos

# edible
## candy land

Board games are fun, but they'd be more fun if they were edible. This one is. The best part: You get to eat whatever you win. Victory is so sweet.

## You will need:

10 graham crackers, broken in half

18 pieces of candy

Peanut butter

Hard candies in different flavors for each player

Single die

[1] Arrange the 20 graham cracker halves in a big S shape on a clean, dry surface. These are the game board spaces. Place pieces of candy on 18 of the crackers and dabs of peanut butter on 2 of them.

[2] Each player chooses a hard candy as a game piece, then rolls the die to see who goes first.

[3] Players roll the die and advance the number of spaces indicated on the die. They get to eat whatever is on the graham crackers they land on (but not the crackers themselves). If they land on a cracker with peanut butter, they're stuck in the Peanut Butter Swamp and can't advance until they roll a six or a one.

[4] Whoever gets to the last graham cracker space first wins and gets to eat whatever candy remains.

# sugar glass

We see right through you: you love your sweets. Your mission is clear: you must mix up a batch of Sugar Glass. Be sure to have an adult supervise—the sugar syrup gets really hot, and you'll need to watch out for stray splatters.

## You will need:

2 cups sugar

⅔ cup white corn syrup

⅔ cup water

Candy thermometer

Food coloring (optional)

½ teaspoon flavor extract (optional)

Baking sheet

1. In a saucepan over medium-high heat, stir together sugar, corn syrup, and water until well blended. Bring to a boil.

[2] Boil until the candy thermometer reaches 300 degrees F. If you don't have a candy thermometer, you'll know it's 300 degrees when a drop of the sugar syrup placed in cold water sounds like breaking glass. Add food coloring and flavor extract if you want colored or flavored Sugar Glass.

[3] Pour syrup into greased baking sheet. Allow to harden. After it sets up, you'll have a pane of edible Sugar Glass. To eat, carefully break off pieces.

*Makes 1 sheet.*

### Variation

**If you'd rather have lollipops than glass, pour syrup into greased ice cube trays instead. After it sets up a bit, insert lollipop sticks (available at baking-supply stores).**

# fudge sludge

It's creamy. It's screamy. It tastes like chocolate and it looks like toxic slime. Do you run away in horror, or do you gobble it down?

### You will need:

14-ounce can sweetened condensed milk

1 tablespoon cornstarch

12 to 15 drops food coloring

½ teaspoon chocolate flavor extract or any other flavor extract you like

[1] Pour sweetened condensed milk into a saucepan over medium heat. Add cornstarch, stirring constantly.

[2] Continue to stir. When the mixture has thickened, remove from heat. Add food coloring and flavor extract.

[3] Allow to cool. Then eat up, if you dare.

*Makes about 2 cups.*

# kitchen sink

## *cookies*

> *Sure, chocolate chip cookies are tasty, but they're not very exciting. These cookies incorporate everything but the kitchen sink. How's that for excitement? You'll need an adult on hand to supervise the oven proceedings.*

### You will need:

1 cup butter or margarine

½ cup brown sugar

½ cup white sugar

1 egg, beaten

¾ teaspoon vanilla extract

1 cup flour

½ teaspoon salt

½ teaspoon baking soda

1½ to 2 cups of add-ins: candy, nuts, oatmeal, peanut butter, or whatever you like

1  Preheat oven to 375 degrees F. In a large bowl, cream together butter or margarine, brown sugar, and white sugar. When the mixture is well blended, add egg and vanilla.

*continued on next page*

[2] In a separate bowl, combine flour, salt, and baking soda. Mix well. Add flour mixture to butter mixture and stir until well-blended.

[3] Stir in your add-ins. Experiment. How do licorice bits, pine nuts, and peanut butter taste together? What about cinnamon, white chocolate chips, and caramel? Sun-dried tomato, banana chips, and wheat germ? Bear in mind that you might want to eat these, though, so don't let your combinations get too gross, unless you have a dog to eat the rejects.

[4] Drop spoonfuls of dough on a cookie sheet, 1 inch apart. Bake for 8 to 10 minutes. Transfer to a rack to cool.

*Makes about 3 dozen cookies.*

blueberry chip cookie

lemon lime swirl cookie

orange creamy dream cookie

## invent your own

# ice cream

*You scream for ice cream, but you want something more exotic than vanilla. Perhaps Prune-Papaya Passion is more your speed, or maybe you're nuts for Goober Grape-nut. Shake up some ice cream with resealable bags, ice, and rock salt and invent your own taste sensation.*

## You will need:

1 gallon-size resealable plastic bag

8 cups ice

1/3 cup rock salt

1 quart-size resealable plastic bag

1 cup whole milk or half-and-half (or a combination of the two)

3 tablespoons sugar

1/4 teaspoon vanilla

Clean, dry pint-sized ice cream container

1/2 cup add-ins: candy, nuts, cereal, cookies, marsh-mallows, chocolate chunks, or whatever you like

9-by-12-inch piece of construction paper

Scissors

Markers

Clear tape

*continued on next page*

[ 1 ] Fill larger plastic bag with ice. Add rock salt.

[ 2 ] Fill smaller plastic bag with milk or half-and-half, sugar, and vanilla. Seal well.

[ 3 ] Place the smaller plastic bag inside the larger plastic bag. Seal well. Shake until the mixture turns into ice cream (about 5 minutes).

[ 4 ] Transfer your ice cream to your container and stir in your add-ins. Be creative. Try peanut butter, marshmallow fluff, and graham crackers. How about pretzels, peanuts, and chocolate chips; toffee bits, caramel, and cashews; jam and chocolate chunks and dried cranberries; or anything you think you might want to eat.

[ 5 ] Come up with a name for your creation. Then make a label from construction paper. Cut paper into two pieces: a circle (3$\frac{1}{2}$ inches in diameter) for the top; and a trapezoid (4 inches wide, 12 inches long at the top, but 11 inches long at the bottom) for the side. Decorate label however you'd like and attach to container with clear tape. Store ice cream in freezer until you're ready to eat it.

*Makes about 2 cups.*

## Instant Gratification Variation

**If you don't have time to Invent Your Own Ice Cream, you can use store-bought vanilla (or whatever flavor you like) and just mix in your custom add-ins.**

# Swamp Cake

Dirt cake with worms and a pond scum glaze—sounds delicious, doesn't it? You don't have to be the Creature from the Black Lagoon to love this creepy cake. It looks disgusting, but you'll go buggy for it.

## You will need:

Chocolate cake mix

½ cup margarine

½ cup evaporated milk

1 teaspoon vanilla extract

12 to 15 drops green food coloring

1-pound box of powdered sugar

Gummi worms and bugs

[1] Bake chocolate cake according to directions on package. Allow to cool.

continued on next page

[2] In a saucepan over medium heat, melt margarine. Add evaporated milk and heat until warm. Remove from heat. Add vanilla extract, food coloring, and powdered sugar. Mix well.

[3] Frost cake while the glaze is still warm. Make it look as goopy as possible.

[4] Decorate with Gummi worms and bugs. Then serve to your horrified friends.

*Makes 10 servings.*

# banana · slugs

> Banana Slugs must be nature's oddest invention: really, really gross and really, really cool at the same time. These banana-flavored candies are a tribute to our favorite gastropod.

## You will need:

⅓ cup margarine or butter (softened)

⅓ cup light corn syrup

Pinch of salt

½ teaspoon banana flavor extract

12 to 15 drops yellow food coloring

3 cups powdered sugar plus more as needed

Wax paper

[1] In a large bowl, beat together margarine or butter, corn syrup, salt, banana flavor extract, food coloring, and powdered sugar. Mix well. If dough is too soft to handle, add more powdered sugar. If it's still too soft, refrigerate until it firms up.

continued on next page

[2] Dust your hands with powdered sugar. Break off
a piece of dough about the size of a golf ball.
Roll into a slug shape between your palms.

[3] Place completed slugs on wax paper and
refrigerate until you're ready to serve them.

*Makes about 30 slugs.*

# fortune cookies

Aren't fortune cookies the best? They provide a taste treat and dispense wisdom. Make a batch yourself, and you can customize your cookies with kooky fortunes. You'll need an adult to supervise the hot cookie handling. Then chow down. Crafty Girl Says: good snacking brings good fortune.

## You will need:

Pen

20 strips of paper, ½ inch wide and 2 inches long

1 cup flour

½ cup sugar

2 tablespoons cornstarch

⅓ cup oil

3 egg whites

¼ cup water

¾ teaspoon vanilla

Aluminum foil

Nonstick cooking spray

*Your true love will look like a m*

*Your lucky number is 2*

continued on next page

Your true love will have double-jointed

You will discover tr... ...ile in a bowl of Alpha-Bits

An albino hamster will bring you

[1] Write fortunes on the 20 slips of paper. Make them as funny, crazy, or cryptic as you'd like.

[2] Preheat oven to 300 degrees F. In a large bowl, combine flour, sugar, and cornstarch. Add oil, egg whites, water, and vanilla and mix until well blended.

[3] Line a baking sheet with aluminum foil. Spray foil with nonstick cooking spray. Then drop teaspoons of batter onto the foil, 5 inches apart. With a spoon, spread each glob of batter into a 4-inch circle.

An act of kindness will be repaid in a thousand c... ...y bars

The family pet loves you best

[4] Bake for 15 to 20 minutes, until the cookies just start to brown. Then get ready to work quickly, because the cookies harden 15 seconds after they come out of the oven.

[5] Remove one cookie from the oven with a spatula. Place a fortune in the center and fold cookie in half. Then fold again so the points touch to make a fortune cookie-shape. You may need to press the cookie against the kitchen counter to get it to bend. Don't press too hard, though, or the cookie will break. Place completed cookie in a muffin tin to cool. Repeat with the rest of the batter.

*Makes 20 cookies*

You will make your fortune from granola bars

You will wear your Wednesday underwear on

s you luck all day

Bananas for breakfast will

Your secret admirer wears green shoes